DK eyewonder
Airplanes

LONDON, NEW YORK,
MELBOURNE, MUNICH, and DELHI

DK UK

Written and edited by Caroline Stamps
Senior art editor Rachael Grady
US editor Margaret Parrish
Producer (print production) Rita Sinha
Producers (pre-production)
Francesca Wardell, Rachel Ng
Jacket designer Natasha Rees
Publisher Andrew Macintyre
Consultant Simon Mumford

DK INDIA

Project art editor Deep Shikha Walia
Assistant editor Deeksha Saikia
Senior editor Priyanka Nath
Senior art editor Rajnish Kashyap
Managing editor Alka Thakur Hazarika
Managing art editor Romi Chakraborty
Senior DTP designer Jagtar Singh
DTP designer Anita Yadav
Picture researcher Sumedha Chopra

First American Edition, 2013
Published in the United States by
DK Publishing
375 Hudson Street
New York, New York 10014

13 14 15 16 17 10 9 8 7 6 5 4 3 2 1
001–187824–06/13

Copyright © 2013 Dorling Kindersley Limited
All rights reserved

Without limiting the rights under copyright reserved
above, no part of this publication may be reproduced,
stored in or introduced into a retrieval system, or
transmitted, in any form, or by any means (electronic,
mechanical, photocopying, recording, or otherwise),
without the prior written permission of both the copyright
owner and the above publisher of this book.
Published in Great Britain by Dorling Kindersley Limited.

A catalog record for this book is available
from the Library of Congress.

ISBN 978-1-4654-0251-6

DK books are available at special discounts when
purchased in bulk for sales promotions, premiums, fund-
raising, or educational use. For details, contact:
DK Publishing Special Markets, 375 Hudson Street,
New York, New York 10014 or SpecialSales@dk.com.

Color reproduction by Scanhouse, Malaysia
Printed and bound in China by Hung Hing

Discover more at
www.dk.com

Contents

Dreams of flight

People have long dreamed of flight, but it took thousands of years before a flying machine was developed that could escape the Earth's gravity and travel up and through the air.

Five hundred years ago

Sketches show that Italian artist and scientist Leonardo da Vinci had put some thought into ways that people might fly. His notebooks contain a series of drawings for machines called ornithopters that had flapping wings.

Would it have worked?

Models have been constructed from da Vinci's diagrams that have proved the machines could not have flown, mainly because they were too heavy.

Da Vinci's machines were designed to have flapping wings.

Let's fly an ornithopter!

"Ornithopter" means "bird wing." Today, bird-sized ornithopters are seen as toys. There are large ornithopters as well—the *Snowbird* (see page 30) is the most successful.

Studying bird flight

For a long time, people thought that flapping wings were the only way to fly because they had studied bird flight.

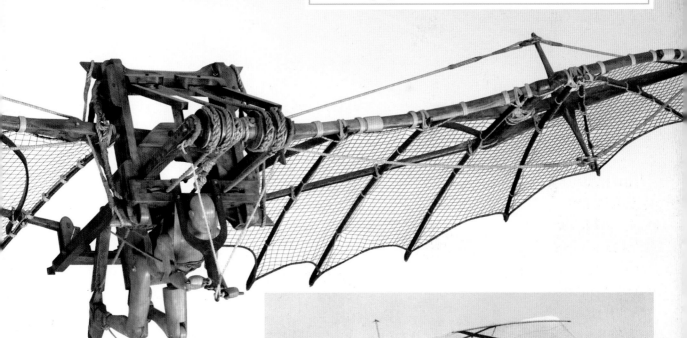

More serious thought

The English engineer Sir George Cayley conducted all kinds of amazing flight tests in the 1800s. He built a glider that carried his coachman across a valley in 1853. Why his coachman? Sir George was 80 by then!

Early gliders

Although some early fliers concentrated their efforts on flapping wing machines, others directed their attention to fixed wings. Known as "the father of flight," German Otto Lilienthal built and flew a number of gliders in the 1890s.

Otto Lilienthal tests one of his gliders in 1891.

How it worked

Lilienthal supported himself on his forearms and controlled the glider by swinging his legs. The wings were made of cotton stretched over a wooden frame.

Flapping wings

Like others before him, Lilienthal studied the flight of birds, publishing *Birdflight As The Basis of Aviation* in 1889. He firmly believed that the secret of powered flight lay in imitating birds.

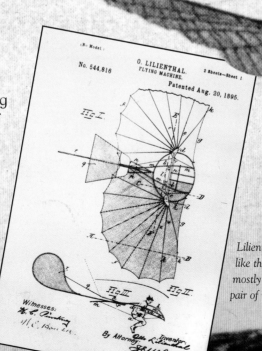

Lilienthal's designs, like this sketch of his, mostly included a single pair of wings.

Hang gliders today

Today's hang gliders are made from light metals and their wings are covered with man-made fabric (a special polyester that is lighter and stronger than cotton).

Glider facts

● In 1893, Lilienthal built a hill he called *Fliegeberg* (Flight Mountain), from which he launched his gliders.

● Lilienthal made about 2,000 flights before he was killed in an accident.

Lilienthal was able to achieve a maximum flight distance of about 1,150 ft (350 m).

A sad end

Lilienthal's work was dangerous. He was killed in an accident in 1896 when he lost control of his glider in a gust of wind and dropped 56 ft (17 m) to the ground.

First flights

On a cold December morning in 1903, at Kitty Hawk, North Carolina, a gas-engined flying machine rose into the air and flew 120 ft (37 m)—less than the length of a jumbo jet. The age of powered flight had begun.

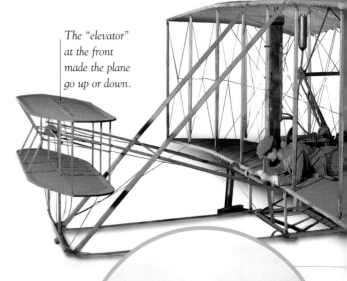

The "elevator" at the front made the plane go up or down.

The Wright brothers

The flying machine had been developed by Orville and Wilbur Wright and was known as the *Wright Flyer*. It was made of wood and fabric.

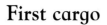

First cargo

The Wright brothers started their flying experiments with kites and moved on to gliders. In 1900, they used a 10-year-old boy, Tom Tate (left), for one of their glider test flights, although the glider was tethered to the ground for the "flight."

The Wright Flyer *achieved the three most important elements of flight—lift, power, and control.*

First flight facts

- The *Wright Flyer* flew just four times before it crashed and was destroyed.

- Tom Tate's mother used the fabric from the discarded 1900 glider's wings to make dresses.

- The *Wright Flyer* had a 12-hp engine. Today, family cars have engines that are 10 times more powerful.

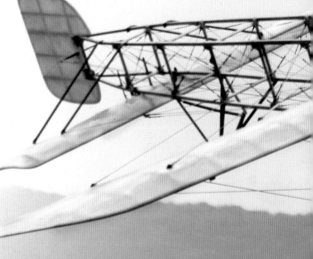

This monoplane is a replica (or copy) of a Blériot XI. One like this was first flown across the English Channel by Louis Blériot.

Turned by the engine, a two-bladed propeller pushed the plane through the air.

The pilot used a system of wires, levers, and pulleys to bend or warp the wing and turn the plane left or right.

IT'S NOT POSSIBLE!

The importance of the *Wright Flyer* was not really understood at the time. Notably, Orville Wright once said, "No flying machine will ever fly from New York to Paris." In fact, this happened just 18 years later.

Quick progression

Advances in flight happened quickly, and the Wright brothers' flights inspired many French aviators in particular. In 1909, Frenchman Louis Blériot was the first person to fly across the English Channel, from France to England.

Gliders

A glider has no engine, so the body is usually sized just large enough to hold the wings and have space for the pilot. So how can it fly if it has no engine to provide power? Gliders use rising pockets of warm air called thermals to fly.

One-piece hinged canopy

Single-seat cockpit

Hole for nose-mounted tow line

Designed to fly
Gliders are designed to fly as efficiently as possible. With a good pilot and the right weather conditions, they can stay in the air for hours at a time.

The main wheel is pulled into the fuselage to make the glider more streamlined.

The highest a glider

The record for the longest glider flight is 1,530 miles (2,463 km), a flight that took 14 hours, 20 minutes.

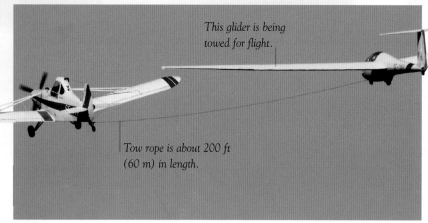

This glider is being towed for flight.

Tow rope is about 200 ft (60 m) in length.

Eased into the air
A glider has to be towed or winched into the air. If towed, it is taken up by a powered plane. Once high enough, the tow line is released and the glider is free to soar.

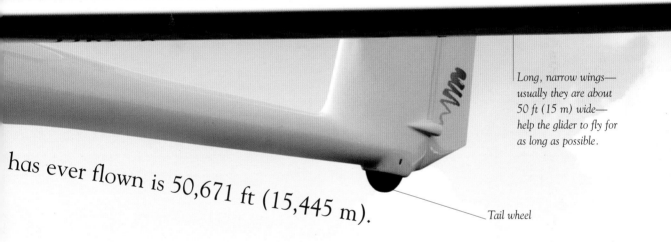

Why are the wings so long?

All wings lose lifting power at the tip because air flowing underneath curls over the top. A long wing helps to reduce this effect and so gives the best possible lift. It makes the plane very efficient (although less maneuverable).

Long, narrow wings—usually they are about 50 ft (15 m) wide—help the glider to fly for as long as possible.

has ever flown is 50,671 ft (15,445 m).

Tail wheel

What are thermals?

Thermals are columns of rising air. A glider pilot uses them to lift the plane in the air. They form over dark patches of ground (which are warmer) and are topped by white, fluffy cumulus clouds. The pilot flies in tight circles to keep inside the thermal and gain height (altitude).

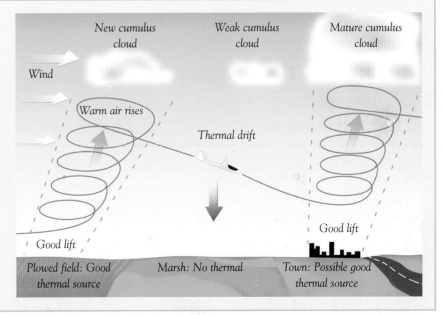

New cumulus cloud

Weak cumulus cloud

Mature cumulus cloud

Wind

Warm air rises

Thermal drift

Good lift

Good lift

Plowed field: Good thermal source

Marsh: No thermal

Town: Possible good thermal source

Biplanes

In the early days of flight, the most common aircraft were planes with two pairs of wings, called biplanes. Biplanes were thought to be safer and they took to the skies in huge numbers during World War I. They were the main aircraft design for the next 20 years.

Most early biplanes had wooden frames covered with fabric. Metal planes were found to be too heavy and too difficult to build until the mid-1930s.

Goggles worn by pilots of the British Royal Flying Corps during World War I

Collar could be folded up to keep neck warm.

Sheepskin-lined leather gloves

Early fighters

World War I broke out in 1914, and it soon became clear that planes would be useful. At first they were used for observation only, but they quickly developed into fighters. The need for ever faster, more maneuverable planes led to incredibly fast developments in aircraft design.

World War I British pilot's gear

Thick rubber sole for good grip

It's cold up there!

Early flights in open cockpits were very cold for pilots. British pilots were issued leather coats for flying, but these were soon replaced by one-piece suits made of waxed cotton and lined with silk and fur.

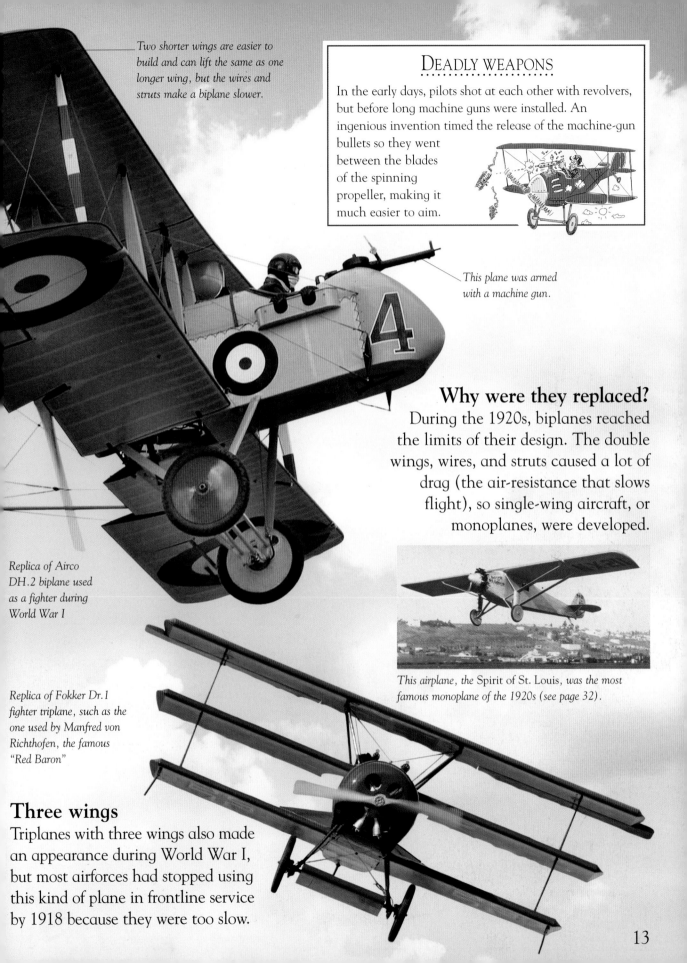

Two shorter wings are easier to build and can lift the same as one longer wing, but the wires and struts make a biplane slower.

DEADLY WEAPONS

In the early days, pilots shot at each other with revolvers, but before long machine guns were installed. An ingenious invention timed the release of the machine-gun bullets so they went between the blades of the spinning propeller, making it much easier to aim.

This plane was armed with a machine gun.

Why were they replaced?

During the 1920s, biplanes reached the limits of their design. The double wings, wires, and struts caused a lot of drag (the air-resistance that slows flight), so single-wing aircraft, or monoplanes, were developed.

Replica of Airco DH.2 biplane used as a fighter during World War I

This airplane, the Spirit of St. Louis, was the most famous monoplane of the 1920s (see page 32).

Replica of Fokker Dr.1 fighter triplane, such as the one used by Manfred von Richthofen, the famous "Red Baron"

Three wings

Triplanes with three wings also made an appearance during World War I, but most airforces had stopped using this kind of plane in frontline service by 1918 because they were too slow.

Monoplanes

Single-wing planes, or monoplanes, began to appear at the end of World War I and proved to be far faster than biplanes. The quest for speed drove engineers to make rapid improvements in the way planes were built in the 1920s and 1930s.

The trophy has been on display since 1977 in London, England.

Getting faster

Between 1913 and 1931, a seaplane air-race called the Schneider Trophy encouraged huge advances in aircraft design. Average speeds for the 11 races that were held increased from 45 mph (73 kph) to 340 mph (547 kph).

Some air raids during World War II saw more than 1,000 aircraft in the skies at one time.

At the start of World War II, countries built huge air forces, and the demands of war improved airplane technology.

Air fights

In 1940, the Spitfires and Hurricanes of the British Royal Air Force fought the Heinkels and Messerschmitts of the German Luftwaffe in what became known as the Battle of Britain.

Shark attack!

The American P-40 Warhawk went into combat during World War II. Many of these aircraft were painted with an eye-catching shark's mouth decoration.

The P-40 Warhawk used a powerful 12-cylinder liquid-cooled engine.

Air armadas

At the height of World War II, bombers were made in huge numbers. They were designed to travel long distances with a heavy bomb load and were equipped with machine guns and turrets to defend themselves from enemy fighters.

The Boeing B-17G Flying Fortress had 13 defensive machine guns.

The first jets

By the end of World War II, the first jet engines had been invented. These allowed planes to go much faster than they had previously. Before long, airplane designers were trying to break the "sound barrier."

The Messerschmitt 262A was the first fully operational, jet-powered aircraft.

Jet planes

The development of the jet engine brought big changes for aircraft because jet planes can fly far faster and higher than propeller-driven planes.

Head-up displays (HUDs)

Jets fly so fast that it can be dangerous for a pilot to look down at the instrument panel and up again. This is why head-up displays were developed to display information directly in front of the pilot.

The jet turbofans of this plane are undergoing maintenance work.

That's a turbine!

Turbine engines burn fuel and air to spin a series of fan blades (the turbine). There are different types, the most common being the turbofan engine.

Jet fighters

Jet planes are widely used as fighter planes because of their speed and maneuverability.

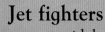

Eject!

The use of ejection seats in jet fighter planes has saved thousands of lives. An ejection seat is fired into the air before a parachute opens—it is so effective that it will even save a pilot if operated at ground level.

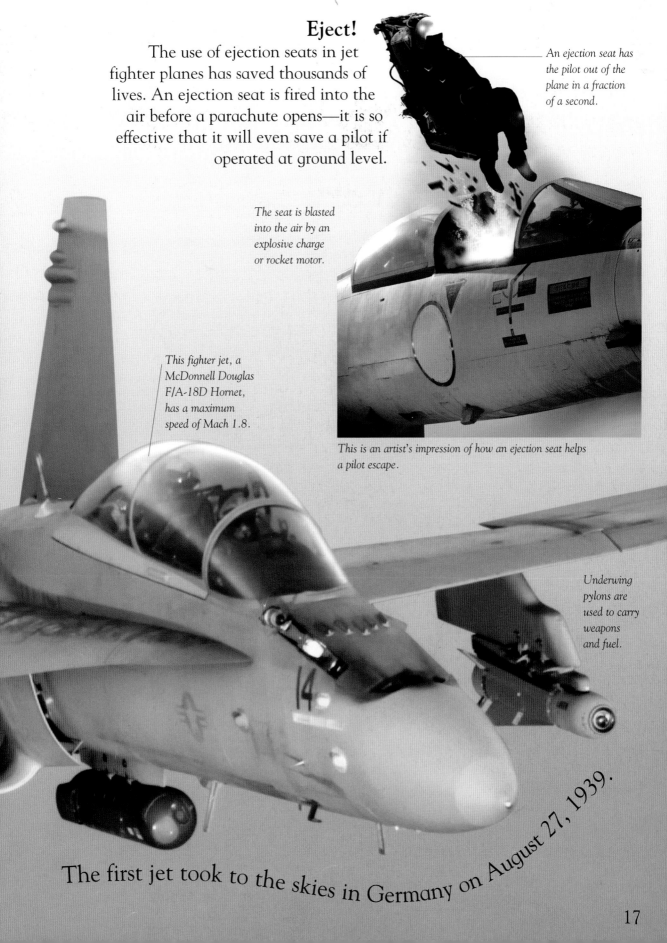

An ejection seat has the pilot out of the plane in a fraction of a second.

The seat is blasted into the air by an explosive charge or rocket motor.

This fighter jet, a McDonnell Douglas F/A-18D Hornet, has a maximum speed of Mach 1.8.

This is an artist's impression of how an ejection seat helps a pilot escape.

Underwing pylons are used to carry weapons and fuel.

The first jet took to the skies in Germany on August 27, 1939.

Passenger planes

The Airbus A380 is the world's largest passenger airplane. It can carry more than 850 people, as well as enough fuel to fill more than 5,300 family cars. Everything about this plane is big.

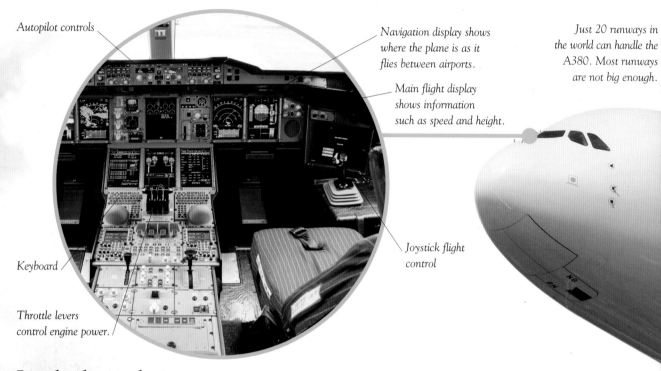

Autopilot controls

Navigation display shows where the plane is as it flies between airports.

Main flight display shows information such as speed and height.

Just 20 runways in the world can handle the A380. Most runways are not big enough.

Joystick flight control

Keyboard

Throttle levers control engine power.

Inside the cockpit
Modern airliners have computer screens and fly-by-wire controls that make them much easier to fly. Autopilot and automatic landing systems make it possible for the aircraft to fly itself for much of the time.

It has been estimated that worldwide about 500,000 people are in the air at any one time.

Let's look inside
Airbus passengers are seated on two levels that run the length of the plane. There are 10 seats in each row on the lower deck and eight seats in each row on the upper deck.

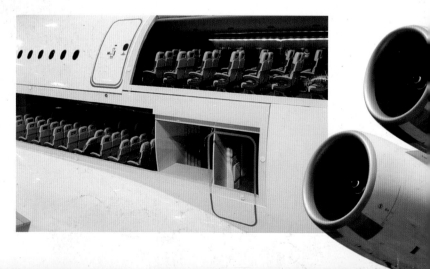

Putting it together

Parts for the Airbus are made all over the world, with the main contractors in France, Germany, Britain, and Spain. The parts are sent to an assembly plant in Toulouse, France, to be put together.

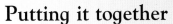

An Airbus wing is moved by road on the first part of its journey from north Wales, UK, to Toulouse, France.

The cockpit section of a superjumbo Airbus is transported on a barge from Hamburg, Germany.

Some parts are delivered in the specially built Beluga cargo plane (see page 36).

The total length of this plane is just under 240 ft (73 m).

Airbus facts

● The Airbus can travel 9,500 miles (15,400 km) without needing to stop and refuel.

● The plane weighs 615 tons (560 metric tons) at takeoff.

● It can carry 85,000 gallons (320,000 liters) of fuel.

● The A380 costs a whopping $390 million.

At the airport

An airport is a busy place, with airplanes constantly arriving and departing. Take a look at a little of what goes on at a busy airport, from gate to takeoff.

Control tower

A pilot is in constant radio contact with the people in the control tower who use radar and computers to make sure all the aircraft keep a safe distance apart.

Ready for takeoff

At some airports, planes take off every minute. They sometimes have to line up and then wait for permission to move, or taxi, onto the runway.

In safe hands

Large airports have their own fire stations. An airport fire engine carries more water and foam than an ordinary fire engine— these trucks fight fires with foam.

The foam cannon on the roof can be controlled from inside the cab.

Go to your gate!

At a large airport, the planes line up at parking places called gates. This is where the passengers get on and off.

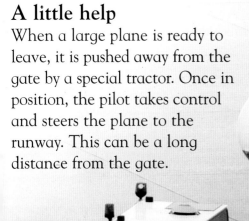

A little help

When a large plane is ready to leave, it is pushed away from the gate by a special tractor. Once in position, the pilot takes control and steers the plane to the runway. This can be a long distance from the gate.

An airliner is being pushed back from the gate.

Supersonic

For years, pilots struggled to control their planes when they got close to the speed of sound (750 mph/1,196 kph). This fearsome sound "barrier," known as Mach 1, was crossed by the X-planes, an experimental series of aircraft built to break all previous records.

Bell X-1

Rocket man

The rocket-powered Bell X-1, flown by fighter pilot Charles "Chuck" Yeager, was the first plane to break the sound barrier. On October 14, 1947, Yeager traveled at 807 mph (1,299 kph). Bell X-1 was launched in the air from beneath a larger plane.

The Concorde's nose lifted in flight to improve streamlining and reduce drag. It was lowered for takeoff and landing to let the pilots see more clearly.

Faster than a bullet

The Concorde was an amazing supersonic passenger airliner. First flown in 1969, it could carry 100 passengers at twice the speed of sound—1,354 mph (2,179 kph), which is faster than a bullet. That works out to 1 mile (1.6 km) every 2.5 seconds!

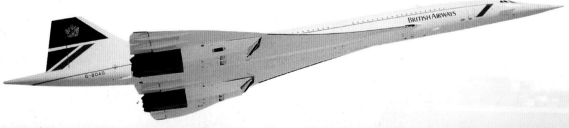

Supersonic planes push aside air with great force. This produces a conical shock wave of pressurized air that moves outward, creating a sonic boom.

Sonic boom!

When a plane travels faster than the speed of sound it creates a shock wave that makes a loud noise. This is a sonic boom. A smaller example of this is the crack of a whip, which occurs because the tip travels faster than the speed of sound and so creates a mini sonic boom.

Space planes of the future may reach speeds of Mach 15!

A peek inside

The Concorde was designed to carry passengers, but it had to be a slim design. This made it narrow inside, so it seated just four people across the cabin.

Jump jet

The Harrier "jump jet" earned its nickname
because it can take off, hover, and land
like a helicopter, but it can fly
as fast as a jet fighter.
It's an amazing plane.

Outrigger landing gear
under the wings for stability

A flying bed

Early designs for the jump jet's
engines and controls were tested in
1953 in a scary-looking contraption
known as the flying bedstead.

The exhaust nozzles
can rotate.

The flying bedstead was tethered to the ground during
its early flights.

How it works

A special engine was designed with four
exhaust nozzles that rotate to point straight
down to lift the plane off the ground and
then point backward to push the plane
along. Once it is going fast enough, the
wings carry the weight of the plane.

The next generation

A new fighter plane called the Lockheed Martin F-35B Lightning is being designed to replace the Harrier. The F-35B can reach supersonic speeds and is also designed to be "stealthy," which makes it harder to see on radar.

Going up

Harriers can take off straight up (VTOL—Vertical takeoff and landing) or use a short takeoff run (V/STOL—Vertical and/or short takeoff and landing) to save fuel and carry more weapons.

Ski jump

Taking off vertically uses a lot of power and fuel so a "ski jump" was invented to give the plane a boost into the sky. Pilots use a short takeoff run and fly off the end of the ramp, which is usually installed on a type of ship called an aircraft carrier.

A Sea Harrier taking off using a ski jump

Aircraft carrier with a ski jump ramp at the forward end of its deck

Seaplanes

Some planes are designed to land on water. They have floats instead of wheels, or streamlined, waterproof hulls. An open stretch of water becomes their runway.

Golden age of flying boats

In the 1930s, flying boats such as the Short S.23 were the only way for passengers to fly to places such as Africa that had very few runways at the time.

Grumman G-21 Goose

This amphibious plane is a modern version of a plane that was originally designed for the residents of Long Island, New York. An aircraft like this was used to carry cargo for many air forces during World War II.

The fuselage provided a lot of space for cargo.

Seaplane words

Seaplanes Flying boats and floatplanes have floats and can land on water.

Amphibious aircraft This is another type of seaplane with a watertight hull and foldable wheels so it can land on either water or land.

Free to land

Seaplanes are widely used in rugged places such as northern Canada, where it can be difficult to build airstrips. These planes can easily operate from rivers or lakes.

A plane that skis!

In areas where there is ice and snow, planes can be equipped with skis to stop them from sinking into the surface when landing and taking off.

A plane equipped with skis prepares to land in Alaska.

HH 3-F Pelican is a specially adapted amphibious helicopter used by the Italian Air Force.

What a flyer!

Amphibians are versatile aircraft that can perform a range of tasks. These include firefighting, air transport in isolated areas, and search and rescue operations.

Floatplanes are usually slower than flying boats because of the extra weight and drag added by their floats.

Helicopters

Ideas for an aircraft that could rise straight into the air were first sketched out some 500 years ago by Italian artist Leonardo da Vinci. However, the first operational helicopter didn't fly until the 1930s.

Made of wood, cloth, and string, this is a model of da Vinci's design for an aerial screw, an early version of the helicopter.

"Helicopter" comes from two Greek words that mean "twisted" and "wing."

Why no wings?

A helicopter's rotor blades are its wings. Driven by an engine, they spin about 500 times a minute to lift the helicopter up into the air.

Tail rotor stops helicopter from spinning around.

A helicopter can be equipped with landing skids rather than wheels.

Good for cargo

The Chinook transport helicopter has two engines. The three-blade rotors each have a diameter of 60 feet (18.3 m).

Main rotor provides lift to the helicopter.

Up, down, left, right

A helicopter is far more flexible in flight than a plane. It can hover without moving and go forward, backward, sideways, and straight up and down. It does not need a runway and can fly almost anywhere.

Helicopter landing on top of a building

An agile flyer

A helicopter can achieve tasks that cannot be performed by fixed-wing aircraft. That's why helicopters are used for search and rescue missions, firefighting, construction, tourism, policing, and by the military.

To the rescue

Helicopters are used to lift shipwrecked survivors to safety by lowering a crewman in a harness.

Heavy duty

"Choppers" are also used as aerial cranes, carrying loads to construction sites that are difficult to reach.

Let's take a tour!

Today, helicopters carry tourists to many breathtaking, but hard-to-reach places, such as Mt. Rushmore, South Dakota.

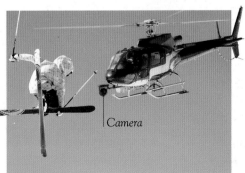

Camera

Extreme filming

Helicopters equipped with filming equipment are often used by movie production companies to capture shots from different angles.

Alternative power

Not all planes are powered by engines. Most people have heard of gliders, but there are also planes that are powered by energy from the Sun, by batteries, and by people.

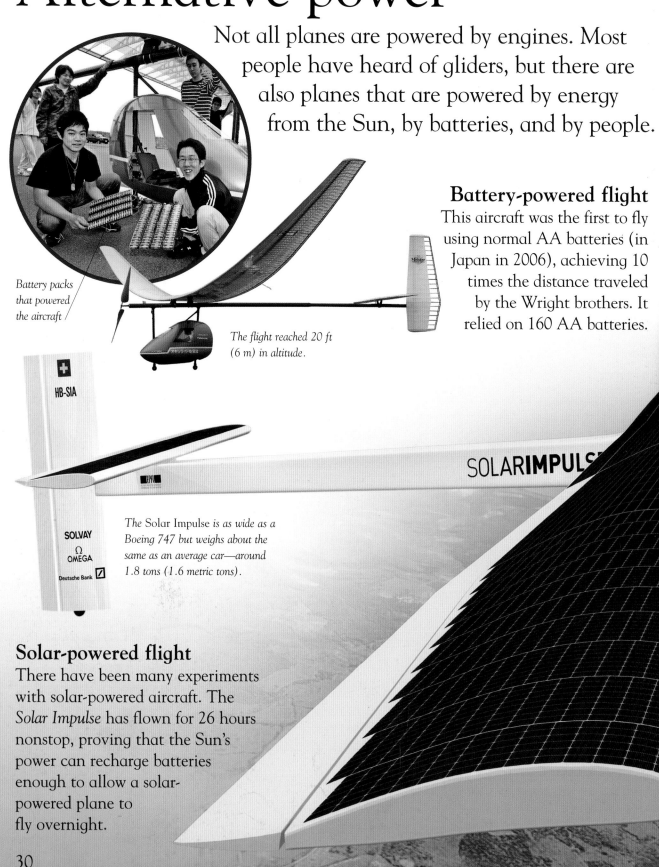

Battery packs that powered the aircraft

Battery-powered flight

This aircraft was the first to fly using normal AA batteries (in Japan in 2006), achieving 10 times the distance traveled by the Wright brothers. It relied on 160 AA batteries.

The flight reached 20 ft (6 m) in altitude.

HB-SIA

SOLVAY
Ω
OMEGA
Deutsche Bank

SOLAR**IMPULSE**

The Solar Impulse is as wide as a Boeing 747 but weighs about the same as an average car—around 1.8 tons (1.6 metric tons).

Solar-powered flight

There have been many experiments with solar-powered aircraft. The *Solar Impulse* has flown for 26 hours nonstop, proving that the Sun's power can recharge batteries enough to allow a solar-powered plane to fly overnight.

Human-powered ornithopter

An ornithopter called the *Snowbird* made a successful human-powered flight in July 2010.

The Snowbird flew for a record of 19.3 seconds, flapping its wings 16 times.

Wingspan is 105 ft (32 m).

The plane's wingspan is 208 ft (63 m).

Pedal power

The Massachusetts Institute of Technology designed and built a human-powered aircraft called *Daedalus* 88. The aircraft flew a record distance of 71 miles (115 km) in April 1988 in Greece.

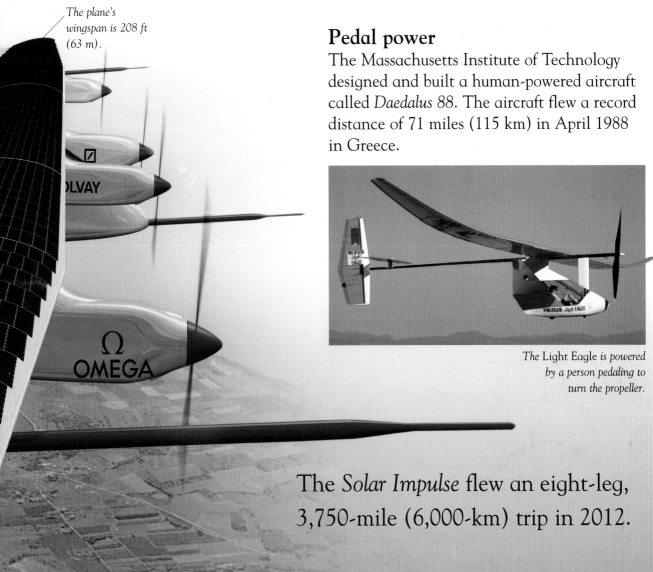

The Light Eagle is powered by a person pedaling to turn the propeller.

The *Solar Impulse* flew an eight-leg, 3,750-mile (6,000-km) trip in 2012.

A famous plane

Perhaps the most famous of all small planes was the *Spirit of St. Louis*, flown by Charles Lindbergh on May 20–21, 1927, on the first nonstop flight from New York to Paris.

Microlights

A microlight is a tiny one- or two-person aircraft with a small engine and a propeller. Some have flexible wings, while others have fixed wings and are more like miniature aircraft.

Let's go fly

People love to fly, and as a result there are a huge variety of small aircraft in the skies today. Let's take a look at some of these.

Metal frame is lightweight aluminum.

The pilot sits in a trike.

The plane's wings are set above the fuselage.

It's a Cessna!

This popular four-seat light aircraft is flown all over the world. It can fly at 137 mph (220 kph).

Yves Rossy, known as the "Rocket Man," steers by using his arms, legs, and head.

I have wings!

Yves Rossy flies using a wing equipped with four mini jet engines, although he starts by jumping from a light plane and lands with a parachute. The fuel allows for about 10 minutes of flying time.

It's in the mail!

It is possible to build a light plane at home. The Zenith XL comes in a box, and is known as a kit plane.

A competitor jumps off the pier.

We can fly!

There are competitions to try and fly a homemade machine as far as possible (over water!). Some of the entries do manage to glide a little way, but most go straight down.

Airshows

Stunt planes are the acrobats of the air. They perform in airshows all over the world, thrilling audiences with skillful aerobatics such as loops, rolls, and spins.

Air races

Racing a plane through the air at high speed around man-made or natural obstacles is an exciting sport that takes place all around the world.

Fast and close

Teams of pilots practice for many hours to display extraordinary skills in the air. The Red Arrows are a world-famous team of nine pilots from the British Royal Air Force.

Fast and furious

Pilots and wing walkers feel positive (+) and negative (–) G-force—the pull of gravity on the body. This picture shows a G-force test. Most pilots can only cope with +8/–6 G for short periods, so the pilot feels 8 x heavier (or 6 x lighter) than he really is.

Smoke trail created by Alpha
Jet aircraft of the French
Acrobatic Patrol team.

Leaving a trail

A special oil is either pumped into the
exhaust or through a separate device to
produce the smoke seen at air shows.
It is sometimes colored with dye.
The smoke leaves a temporary trail in
the sky showing the aircraft's path.

Wing walkers
perform at
high speeds.

GUINOT

Standing on a wing

Wing walking is when a person
stands on top of the wings of a plane
while it flies (they are strapped to the
plane for safety). Biplanes are often
used for wing walking.

ZIP, ZAP, ZOOM!

The first international airshow was held
in 1909 in Reims, France. The fastest
planes there flew at 45 mph (75 kph)
and climbed to just 500 ft (150 m).
Just four years later, airplanes were
flying at more than 120 mph (200 kph)
and reaching 20,000 ft (6,000 m).

Cargo planes

From food to furniture, planes are an essential means of moving goods. All kinds of planes carry goods, but perhaps the strangest looking cargo plane is the Beluga.

Parts for the Beluga come from all over the world: wings from the UK, tail and doors from Spain, fuselage from Germany, and nose from France.

Hinged cargo door opens from top.

I RECOGNIZE THAT SHAPE

With its bulky fuselage, the Airbus Beluga looks as if it shouldn't fly. It was originally called the Super Transporter, but became known as the Beluga, after the beluga whale, because of its shape.

Open wide

That front hides a secret—it opens to reveal a huge, cavelike interior. The transporter plane carries both large aircraft parts and International Space Station components.

Moving a spaceship

When the Space Shuttle needed to be moved from place to place it was given a piggyback ride on top of a specially adapted Boeing 747.

There are currently five Belugas in operation with Airbus.

A huge door

In this older version of the Beluga, the front section is hinged to open to one side. The plane has a 25-ft- (7.6-m-) wide fuselage. Rails and rollers in the loading bay make it easy to load cargo.

Another giant

The world's heaviest aircraft is the military transporter Antonov AN-225, an enlarged version of the Antonov AN-124, shown below. The AN-225 can carry 250 tons (226.7 metric tons), unlike the Beluga's 47 tons (42.6 metric tons).

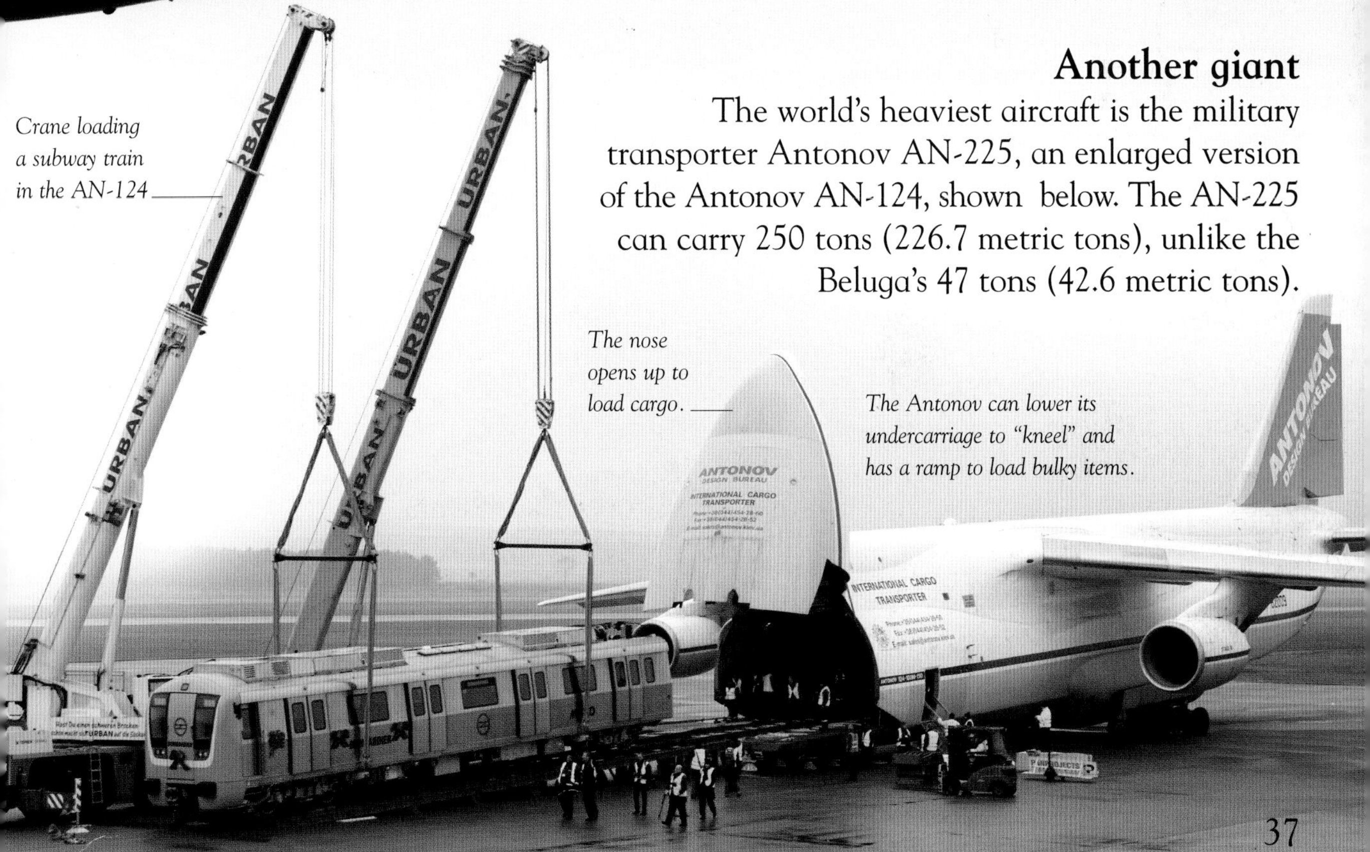

Crane loading a subway train in the AN-124

The nose opens up to load cargo.

The Antonov can lower its undercarriage to "kneel" and has a ramp to load bulky items.

Fight that fire

A water bomber swoops down to scoop up water from a lake, then heads to drop its load on a raging fire. Planes—and helicopters—play a vital role in fighting forest fires.

The wings and engines are high to keep them clear of the water's surface.

One of these planes has made an amazing 225 water drops in a day.

Bombardier 415

● The plane has four tanks. Twelve full loads would fill a swimming pool.

● It is able to take off and land in water, even if the waves are 4 ft (1.2 m) high.

● It takes 12 seconds to scoop up 1,600 gallons (6,100 liters) of water.

● The plane can scoop from water as shallow as 6½ ft (2 m).

Water pickup

Some firefighting planes are able to scoop up and drop water onto a forest fire. They carry huge loads and can return to reload again and again.

Why is it red?

A colored chemical known as a fire retardant is sometimes added to show pilots areas they have covered as well as helping to stop the water from dispersing in a fine mist as it drops.

The red liquid contains fertilizer, gum Arabic, red iron oxide, and water to slow and cool the fire. The fertilizer helps new growth.

US 747 Supertanker

A firefighter fills an airtanker with fire retardant.

Preloaded

Not all firefighting planes scoop up water. Airtankers are filled at an airport and fly to the site of a fire. Different planes can be converted into airtankers. There is even a supertanker—a converted Boeing 747—that holds a massive 20,500 gallons (77,600 liters). It's the world's largest aerial firefighting plane.

Firefighting helicopter

This helicopter picks up water through a 26-ft- (8-m-) long snorkel, refilling its massive tank in just 45 seconds. Helicopters can hover to target a specific area of a fire, dropping their load in just three seconds.

Snorkel

Into space

Advances in flight made people dream of reaching space. In the 1960s, President John F. Kennedy announced that the United States would land astronauts on the Moon before 1970. This happened in July 1969, and since then an amazing number of spacecraft have been launched.

Ready for next time

First launched in 1981, the Space Shuttle was unique because it was the only spacecraft that could travel into space and return to Earth on repeat journeys.

The Space Shuttle

The Space Shuttle was made up of four main parts. The Orbiter/Space Shuttle required a gigantic fuel tank and two booster rockets to blast it up into space. The last shuttle made its final flight in 2011.

In over 27 years of service, Space Shuttle Discovery completed 39 successful missions.

Space facts

● Unmanned probes launched in the late 1970s are just leaving our solar system.

● Twelve people have now landed on the Moon.

● Each shuttle was built to achieve about 100 missions.

● It took just 8½ minutes for a space shuttle to reach space.

Satellites

All kinds of satellites orbit the Earth. They were blasted into space with the help of rockets, or taken up by the Space Shuttle. They help to provide information about the Earth.

In 2002, satellite Envisat was launched to obtain detailed information on global warming and climatic changes. It ceased operations in April 2012.

Living in space

Space stations orbit the Earth and allow astronauts to live in space, conducting experiments and servicing satellites.

The International Space Station photographed from Space Shuttle Atlantis on November 25, 2009.

Controls at the end of armrest

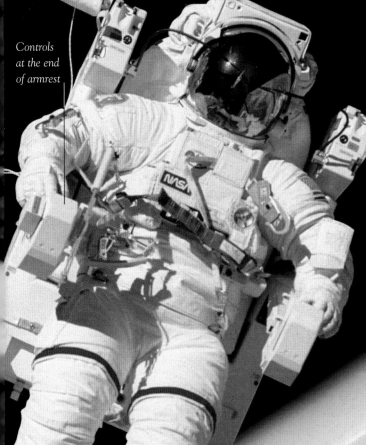

The space suit has 24 tiny rocket motors.

A flight in space

An astronaut is shown using an MMU (Manned Maneuvering Unit). Only a handful of untethered "flights" in space have been made.

Astronauts eat a snack while they float freely inside the International Space Station.

A look at a plane

You can probably name the main parts of an airplane, but do you know where the ailerons and elevators are and what they do? Let's take a closer look at a typical light aircraft.

On larger planes the cockpit is also known as the flight deck.

The control panel

Cockpits vary, depending on the plane. The image to the left shows the inside of a Cessna's cockpit. A cockpit contains an instrument panel, and different controls that help the pilot fly the plane.

Strut for extra strength

The plane's wingspan is measured from wingtip to wingtip.

Two-blade propeller

How do they do that?

Pilots are highly trained. It takes a lot of skill to fly an airplane and pilots take years to learn how.

Steerable nose wheel

Main wheel

A plane's body is called the fuselage.

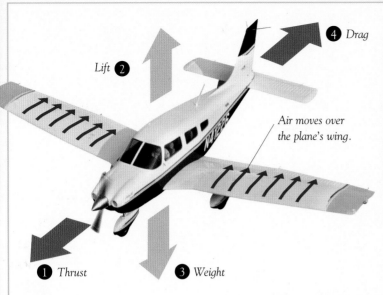

Lift **2**

4 Drag

Air moves over
the plane's wing.

1 Thrust

3 Weight

How a plane flies
Four forces act on a plane.
1 The engine generates thrust that drives the plane forward.
2 When the plane goes fast enough, air going over the wings creates lift.
3 When the lift is greater than the weight, the aircraft will fly.
4 Once in the air, wind resistance tries to hold the plane back. This is called drag.
To keep the plane flying, all of these forces need to be in balance.

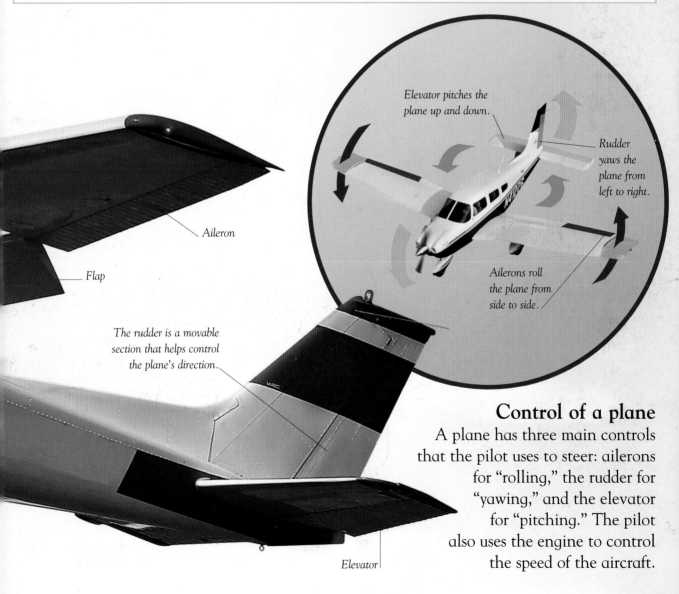

*Elevator pitches the
plane up and down.*

*Rudder
yaws the
plane from
left to right.*

Aileron

Flap

*Ailerons roll
the plane from
side to side.*

*The rudder is a movable
section that helps control
the plane's direction.*

Elevator

Control of a plane
A plane has three main controls that the pilot uses to steer: ailerons for "rolling," the rudder for "yawing," and the elevator for "pitching." The pilot also uses the engine to control the speed of the aircraft.

Aviation records

Let's have a look at some of the record-breaking events in the history of aviation.

1783 The first recorded manned flight lasted for about 25 minutes and took place in a hot-air balloon built by the Montgolfier brothers. The balloon was made from linen lined with paper.

1903 The first controlled, powered airplane flight was achieved by the Wright brothers. The flight lasted just 12 seconds.

1930 Amy Johnson made the first solo England–Australia flight.

1919 This year saw the first England–Australia flight in a Vickers Vimy. It took 135 hours and 55 minutes at an average speed of 82 mph (132 kph).

1941 Gloster E28/39 becomes the first successful jet aircraft.

1931 New speed record set of 407 mph (655 kph)

1783 1903 1906 1912 1919 1927 1930 1931 1932 1933 1941

1906 First recognized speed record of 25 mph (41 kph)

1912 Speed record set of 100 mph (160 kph)

1927 Charles Lindbergh took 33½ hours to complete the first nonstop solo transatlantic flight, flying from New York to Paris, France.

1933 Wiley Post made the first round-the-world solo flight in *Winnie Mae*.

1919 The first nonstop transatlantic flight was made by Alcock and Brown, from St. John's, in Newfoundland, Canada, to Ireland.

1932 Amelia Earhart became the first woman (and the second person) to fly a nonstop solo transatlantic flight. She was also the first person to fly the crossing twice.

1976 The Lockheed SR-71 Blackbird holds the official Air Speed Record for a manned air-breathing jet aircraft with a speed of 2,193 mph (3,530 kph).

2005 Launch of Airbus A380, the largest mass-produced aircraft. The A380 can take more passengers than any other passenger plane, with a maximum capacity of 853 passengers.

1947 Chuck Yeager breaks the sound barrier in the Bell X-1.

1967 An experimental rocket-powered aircraft achieved 4,520 mph (7,273 kph)—nearly seven times the speed of sound. This remains the record for a manned aircraft.

1986 August John Egginton takes the record for the fastest helicopter flight in a Lynx, reaching 249.1 mph (400.87 kph).

| 1947 | 1952 | 1967 | 1969 | 1976 | 1986 | 1988 | 2004 | 2005 | 2012 |

1969 First flight of the Concorde, the world's first supersonic airliner.

1986 December Dick Rutan and Jeana Yeager made the first nonstop, unrefueled fixed-wing aircraft flight around the Earth in the Rutan *Voyager*. They took 9 days, 3 minutes, and 44 seconds.

2004 The unmanned NASA X-43A set a new speed record for an air-breathing aircraft of 6,598 mph (10,617 kph), Mach 9.65.

1952 De Havilland Comet is the world's first jet airliner to enter service.

1988 The Antonov An-225 takes the record for the world's longest and heaviest aircraft.

2005 The first nonstop solo fixed-wing aircraft flight around the Earth was achieved by Steve Fossett on the Virgin Atlantic *GlobalFlyer*. The journey took just over 67 hours.

2012 Felix Baumgartner becomes the first person to break the sound barrier in free fall without a vehicle.

45

True or false?

It's time to test your knowledge of planes. Spot whether these statements are true or false. Get going!

The Wrights brothers' flying machine was called the Wright Machine.
See page 8

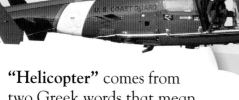

"Helicopter" comes from two Greek words that mean "rotating" and "blade."
See page 28

The *Spirit of St. Louis* was a famous microlight.
See page 32

An ancient Greek myth tells of Daedalus and his son, Icarus, who escaped using wax-and-feather wings.
See page 5

Some people build planes at home. Such planes arrive in a kit form.
See page 33

It's possible to fly by cycle power.
See page 31

Just nine people have traveled to the Moon and back.
See page 40

A plane's wingspan is measured from the wing's leading edge to the trailing edge.
See page 43

Wing walking is when a person walks on the wings of a plane as it flies.
See page 35

The Space Shuttle reached space in less than nine minutes.
See page 40

World tour

Bring your passport and board a plane for this world tour game—but watch out for hazards as you race your friends to reach the finish line.

Winds in your favor. Move forward 6

Land in remote Canadian island to fix a wing. Skip a turn

Clear skies over North America. Roll again

How to play

This game is for up to four players.

You will need

Move down   Move up

A die
Counters—one for each player
Trace over the plane outlines or cut and color your own from cardboard. Each player takes turns rolling the die and begins from the START box. Follow the squares with each roll of the die. If you land on an instruction, make sure you do as it says. Good luck!

Stop to visit a rain forest. Skip a turn

Held up waiting for luggage. Skip a turn

 START

Waiting for clearance to land. **Move back 3**

FINISH How many stamps did you collect in your passport?

European winds blow you off course. **Move back 3**

Cleared to speed through Asia. **Move forward 2**

Give way to migrating birds. **Move back 4**

Cleared to take a shorter route over Australia. **Move forward 5**

Blown along by an Antarctic storm. **Move forward 2**

Snowstorm! Land at the closest airport. **Move back 5**

What's this?

Take a look at these close-ups of some of the pictures in the book and see if you can identify them. The clues will help.

- ✈ This one began life as a sketch 500 years ago.
- ✈ It is a model.
- ✈ Could it fly?

See page 4–5

- ✈ This part rotates.
- ✈ "Jump" is a clue.
- ✈ A vertical takeoff? No problem!

See page 24

- ✈ This plane's nose moves!
- ✈ It's a supersonic jet.
- ✈ The aircraft first flew in 1969.

See page 22–23

- ✈ That's an odd shape!
- ✈ It has an unusual door.
- ✈ This plane can carry a massive load.

See page 36

- ✈ It has spinning blades.
- ✈ Early versions first flew in the 1930s.
- ✈ This aircraft can hover.

See page 28

- ✈ This is a piece of history.
- ✈ Why does it have guns?
- ✈ This is not a biplane, it's a mono_____.

See page 15

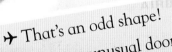

➤ I can land on snow.
➤ I am a small passenger aircraft.
➤ I can ski.

See page 27

➤ It's huge!
➤ How do you control it?
➤ This is the largest passenger plane.

See page 18

➤ Showing off!
➤ We can leave a colorful trail.
➤ This is good entertainment.

See page 34–35

➤ Think "space."
➤ I am not a plane...
➤ ... and yet I can fly!

See page 41

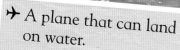

➤ A plane that can land on water.
➤ Is that a float or a wheel?
➤ Is it amphibious?

See page 38

Flight path frenzy

Can you guide the plane along the right flight path from takeoff to landing? Answer the questions correctly to reach the runway.

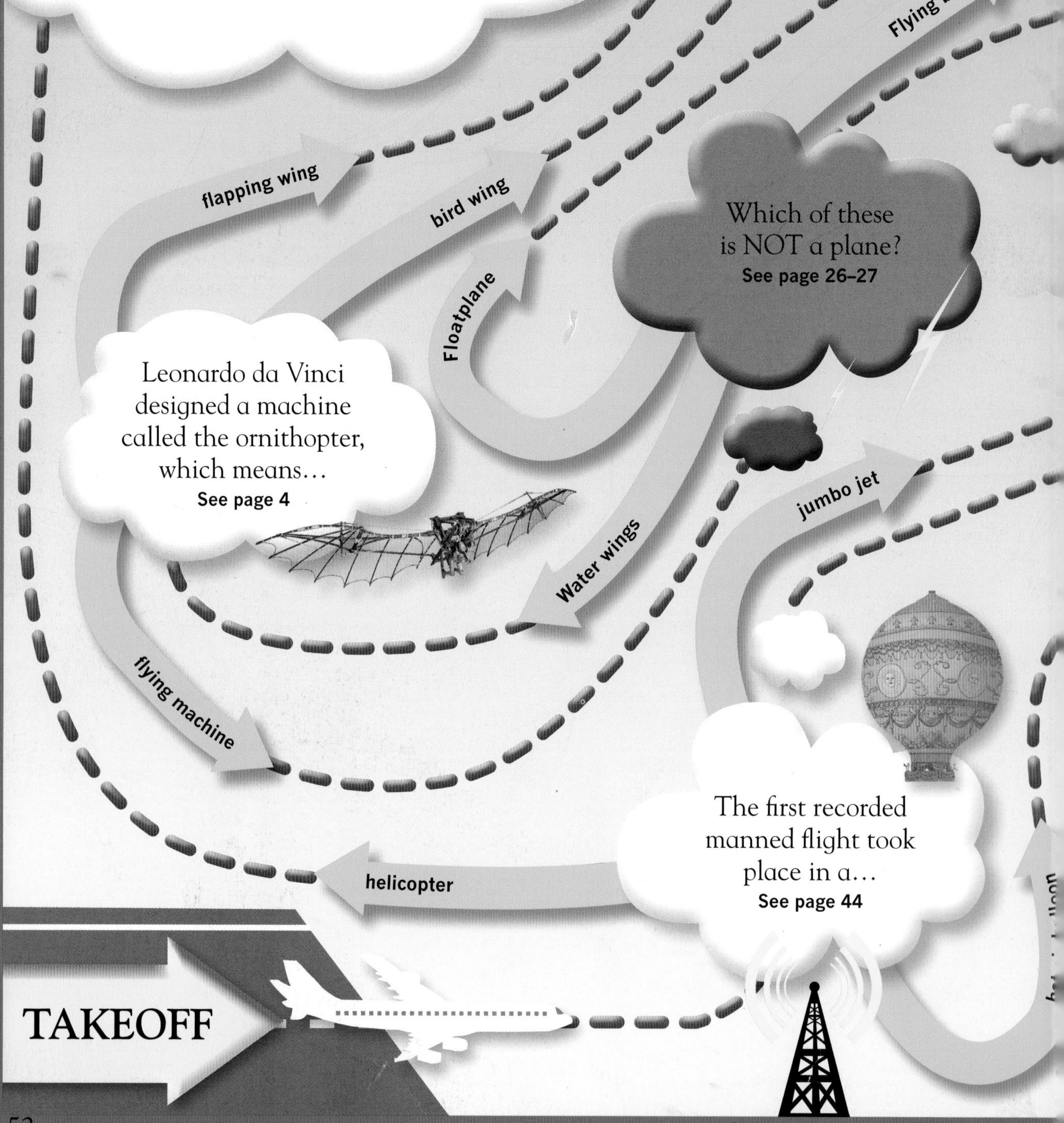

Flying boat

flapping wing

bird wing

Floatplane

Which of these is NOT a plane?
See page 26–27

Leonardo da Vinci designed a machine called the ornithopter, which means…
See page 4

Water wings

jumbo jet

flying machine

helicopter

The first recorded manned flight took place in a…
See page 44

TAKEOFF

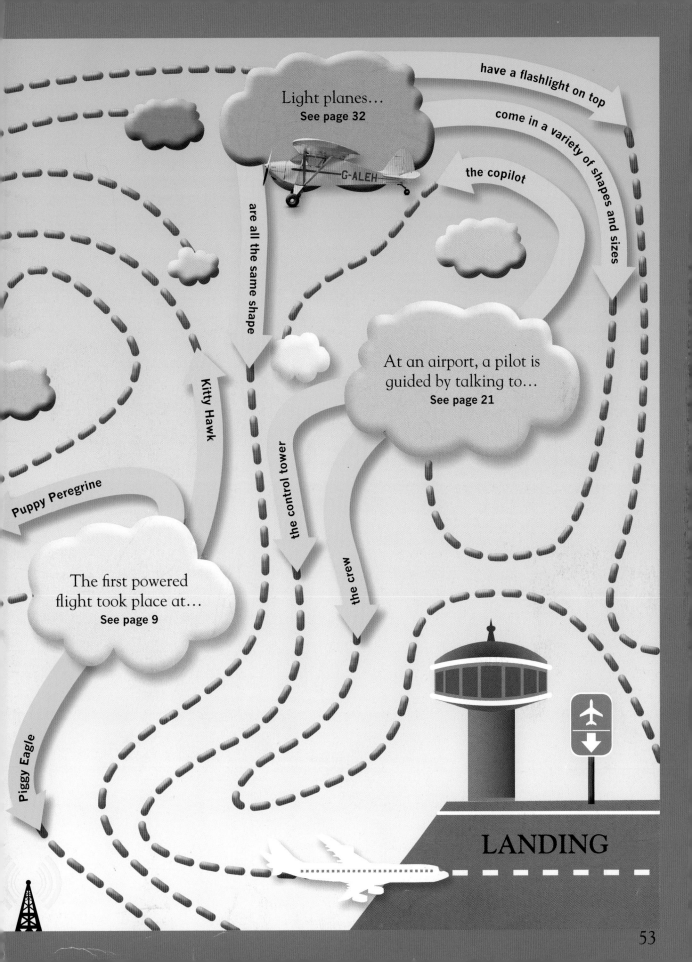

Glossary

The meanings of these words
are useful to know when you are learning
about airplanes.

Ailerons flaps on each end of the wing that roll an airplane from side to side (a movement called "roll").

Altitude the height at which a plane is flying.

Amphibian (airplane) an airplane that can operate on land and water.

Autopilot a computerized system that flies an airplane automatically.

Aviator another name for a pilot.

Biplane an airplane with two wings, one above the other.

Control tower a tall airport building. The people inside direct the aircraft flying into and out of the airport.

Drag the pressure of air slowing an airplane in flight.

Ejection seat this helps a pilot escape from an airplane in an emergency.

Elevator flap on an airplane tail that makes a plane move up or down (a movement called "pitch").

Flap this lowers from the wing to help an airplane fly more slowly.

Flight deck another name for the cockpit of an airplane, where the pilots operate the flight controls.

Fly-by-wire a system that uses computers, electric signals, and motors to help control an airplane.

Fuselage the main body of an airplane that holds the crew, passengers, and baggage or cargo.

G-force the pull of gravity on an airplane and the people inside.

Glider an aircraft that can fly without the use of an engine.

Head-up display (HUD) this displays information directly in front of the pilot.

Jet engine an engine that takes in air from outside, mixes it with fuel, burns it, and pumps it out again to push the aircraft forward.

Joystick control stick, used to "pitch" and "roll" an aircraft.

Lift the force created by air passing over the wing that keeps an airplane flying.

Monoplane a single-wing airplane.

Ornithopter an aircraft with flapping wings.

Propeller the rotating blades on some aircraft. Propellors are driven by engines and power the plane through the air.

Radar a way of using radio to detect objects that are not in sight.

Rudder flap on an airplane tail that helps the pilot turn left or right (a movement called "yaw").

Runway strip of ground where airplanes can take off or land.

Supersonic faster than the speed of sound (which is also known as Mach 1).

Taxi this is when an airplane moves on its wheels on the ground.

Thermal rising body of warm air. A glider uses thermals to stay in the air.

Throttle mechanism on the flight deck that controls the flow of fuel to the plane's engines, which allows the pilot to control the speed.

Thrust the force that drives an airplane forward. It usually comes from either a propellor or jet engine.

Undercarriage another name for a plane's landing gear or wheels.

VTOL this stands for Vertical takeoff and landing.

Index

Acknowledgments

Dorling Kindersley would like to thank:
Andy Cooke for artwork and Fleur Star for assistance with the activity spreads.

Picture credits

The publisher would like to thank the following for their kind permission to reproduce their photographs:

(Key: a-above; b-below/bottom; c-center; f-far; l-left; r-right; t-top)

1 **Alamy Images:** RTimages (c). 2-3 **Dreamstime.com:** Pavel Losevsky. 4 **Getty Images:** Aksaran / Gamma-Rapho (bc). **Mary Evans Picture Library:** (tc). 5 **Dreamstime.com:** Steve ehlenschlager (tc); Howard Sandler (tl). **Philip Jarrett:** (br). 6-7 **Dreamstime.com:** Mauhorng (t). **Getty Images:** Imagno / Hulton Archive (b). 6 **Corbis:** Bettmann (cl). **Getty Images:** Hulton Archive (bc). 7 **Alamy Images:** John Bentley (tl). **Corbis:** Sammlung Sauer / dpa (br). 8 **Corbis:** Bettmann (cr). **Library Of Congress, Washington, D.C.:** Wright Brothers Negatives (cl). 8-9 **Corbis:** Air Classics Gelnhausen / dpa (b). **SuperStock:** Science and Society (tc). 10-11 **Dreamstime.com:** Mauhorng (t). **SuperStock:** imagebroker.net (c). 10 **Dreamstime.com:** Navarone (bl). 12-13 **Dreamstime.com:** Italianestro (Background). **Getty Images:** Jim Tannick / Getty Images Entertainment (c). 13 **Corbis:** Bettmann (crb). **Dreamstime.com:** Vladvitek (bc). 14 **Getty Images:** (tr, b); Science & Society Picture Library (cra). 15 **Alamy Images:** Scott Germain / Stocktrek Images, Inc. (tr); Ilene MacDonald (br). **Corbis:** Phil Klein (cl). 16 **Corbis:** Richard Baker / In Pictures (tr); Peter Ginter / Science Faction (c). 16-17 **Corbis:** Ed Darack / Science Faction (b). 17 **Dreamstime.com:** Philcold (tr). 18 **Alamy Images:** Tony Hobbs (tl); Mark Mercer (c). 19 **Corbis:** Ian Hodgson / Reuters (tc). **Dorling Kindersley:** Christian Charisius / Reuters (ca). **Getty Images:** AP (c); Bloomberg (b). 20 **Corbis:** Koca Little Company / cultura (c); VEM / Westend61 (l). **Dreamstime.com:** Seena5050 (cb). 21 **Corbis:** Richard Michael Pruitt / Dallas Morning News (cl). **Dreamstime.com:** Shutterbas (b). 22 **Corbis:** NASA - digital version copyright / Science Faction (cl). **Dorling Kindersley:** British Airways (b). 22-23 **Alamy Images:** Jerome Yeats (c). 23 **Alamy Images:** Bruce Benedict / Transtock

Inc. (br). **Reuters:** Christopher Pasatieri (tl). 24-25 **Dreamstime.com:** David Acosta Allely (tc). 24 **Dreamstime.com:** David Acosta Allely (cb). **Getty Images:** Science & Society Picture Library (bl). 25 **Corbis:** HO / Reuters (tr). **Reuters:** Handout Old (b). 26 **Alamy Images:** Antony Nettle (cl). **TopFoto.co.uk:** Flight Collection (tr). 26-27 **Corbis:** Robert Garvey (b). 27 **Alamy Images:** Mattia Oselladore (cl). **SuperStock:** Joe Stock / Alaska Stock (tr). 28 **Getty Images:** Leonardo da Vinci / The Bridgeman Art Library (tl). 28-29 **Dreamstime.com:** Ron Hilton (b). 29 **Corbis:** U.S. Coast Guard - - digital ve / Science Faction (ca); Reuters (c); Tom Nebbia / Imaginechina (bl). **Dreamstime.com:** Neil Harrison (bc); Steve Mann (tl). 30 **Getty Images:** Koichi Kamoshida (c); Yoshikazu Tsuno / AFP (tl). 30-31 **Getty Images:** S012 / Solar Impulse Epfl / Gamma-Rapho (b). 31 **NASA:** (crb); Todd Reichert: (t). 32-33 **Alamy Images:** Pics that fly (bc). 32 **Alamy Images:** Colin Underhill (bl). **Getty Images:** New York Times Co. (tl). 33 **Corbis:** Laurent Gillieron / Epa (t). **Getty Images:** AFP (tr); Scott Barbour (br). 34 **Corbis:** Bettmann (bl). **Getty Images:** Andrew Holt / Britain On View (cr); Martin Rose (tl). 34-35 **Corbis:** Ali Hader / epa (bl). 35 **Corbis:** Frédéric Soreau / Photononstop (t). 36-37 **Getty Images:** John Macdougall / AFP (bl). 36-37 **Dreamstime.com:** Brutusman (t). 37 **Corbis:** Bettmann (cra). **NASA:** (t). **TopFoto.co.uk:** Â © ullsteinbild (b). 38 **Dreamstime.com:** Tupungato (tc). **Getty Images:** AFP. 39 **Alamy Images:** ZUMA Press (cl). **Corbis:** Gene Blevins / ZUMA Press (tr). **Getty Images:** Jack Guez / AFP (c). **SuperStock:** Marka (br). 40 **NASA:** (l); (c). 41 **Corbis:** Esa / epa (tr). **NASA:** (br, cr, br/background); Great Images in NASA (l). 42 **Alamy Images:** David R. Frazier Photolibrary, Inc. (cla). 42-43 **Dreamstime.com:** Neil Harrison (b); Italianestro (Background). 43 **Corbis:** Winston Luzier / Transtock (tl, cr). 44 **Corbis:** Bettmann (crb); Library of Congress - digital ve / Science Faction (ca); Underwood & Underwood (cra); Heritage Images (clb). **Getty Images:** Science & Society Picture Library (tl, bc). 44-45 **Dreamstime.com:** Italianestro (Background). 45 **Corbis:** Thomas Frey / dpa (bl); Smithsonian Institution (cla); Redbull / Handout / redbull content pool (crb). **Dreamstime.com:** Steve Mann (cra). **Getty Images:** USAF (tc). 46 **Corbis:** Terraqua Images (cla). **SuperStock:** Science and Society (tr). 47 **Alamy Images:** Susan & Allan Parker (cl). **NASA:** Great Images in NASA (tr). 50-51 **Dreamstime.com:** Brutusman (tc). 50 **Alamy Images:** Jerome Yeats (cr). **Corbis:** Phil Klein (br). **Dreamstime.com:** David Acosta Allely (c); Brutusman (b); Ron Hilton (bc). 51 **Alamy Images:** Mark Mercer (cra). **Corbis:** Frédéric Soreau / Photononstop (cl). **Dreamstime.com:** Tupungato (bl). **NASA:** Great Images in NASA (c). **SuperStock:** Joe Stock / Alaska Stock (tc, br). 54-55 **Dreamstime.com:** Tupungato (b). 56 **Alamy Images:** Richard Cooke (clb). 58 **Corbis:** Terraqua Images (clb). **Dorling Kindersley:** Ted Taylor - modelmaker (br). 59 **Dorling Kindersley:** Edgar Gillingwater - modelmaker (br); Imperial War Museum, Duxford (cra); The Shuttleworth Collection, Bedfordshire (clb). **Photolibrary:** Photodisc / PhotoLink (crb).

All other images © Dorling Kindersley
For further information see: www.dkimages.com